Blind Pumper at the Well

RALPH SALISBURY is of English-Irish-American Indian descent. His writing covers themes from ecology to anti-war protest and support for world brotherhood and sisterhood. He was a volunteer in the US Air Force in WWII, and became an opponent to the Korean War, the Vietnam War and the war in Iraq. His father's father was a Cherokee medicine man. His paternal grandmother was a Cherokee-Shawnee story teller. A natural, self-taught musician with an eloquent voice, Salisbury's father made a living as a traveling minstrel before settling on the Iowa farm, where Salisbury was born.

Earthworks Series

Series Editor: Janet McAdams

KIMBERLY BLAESER: *Apprenticed to Justice*
QWO-LI DRISKILL: *Walking with Ghosts*
HEID E. ERDRICH: *The Mother's Tongue*
DIANE GLANCY: *Rooms: New and Selected Poems*
ALLISON ADELLE HEDGE COKE: *Blood Run*
ALLISON ADELLE HEDGE COKE (ed): *Effigies*
GORDON D. HENRY: *The Failure of Certain Charms and Other Disparate Signs of Life*
LEANNE HOWE: *Evidence of Red: Poems and Prose*
DEBORAH A. MIRANDA: *The Zen of La Llorona*
PHILLIP CARROLL MORGAN: *The Fork-in-the-Road Indian Poetry Store*
PHILIP RED EAGLE: *Red Earth: A Vietnam Warrior's Journey*
CARTER REVARD: *How the Songs Come Down: New and Selected Poems*
CAT RUIZ: *Stirring Up the Water*
RALPH SALISBURY: *Blind Pumper at the Well*
CHERYL SAVAGEAU: *Mother/Land*
JAMES THOMAS STEVENS: *A Bridge Dead in the Water*
GERALD VIZENOR: *Almost Ashore*

Blind Pumper at the Well

Poems from My 80th Year

Ralph Salisbury

Cambridge

PUBLISHED BY SALT PUBLISHING
PO Box 937, Great Wilbraham. Cambridge CB21 5JX United Kingdom

First published 2008

Printed and bound in the United States of America by Lightning Source Inc.

Typeset in Swift 9.5/13

ISBN 978 1 84471 406 3 paperback

Salt Publishing Ltd gratefully acknowledges the financial assistance of Arts Council England

1 3 5 7 9 8 6 4 2

I dedicate this book to my fellow poet and wife of 39 years, Ingrid Wendt; to my children, Jeff, Brian and Martina; to my grandchildren, Connor, Travis and Gemma; and to all of my people, the living and the dead.

Grateful acknowledgment to the following journals and anthologies for first publication of some poems:

Sheep Ranch Near Air Base, in *Dona Nobis Pacem* (*Give Us Peace*)
Two Poems in Memory of Nils-Aslak Valkeapaa, B. 1943, D. 2001, in *Ice Floe*
Peaches in the Pantry, Some Rhymes for Smug Inheritors,
in *Street Magazine*
Student Writing, in *Southwest Review*

Contents

SECTION ONE

(SAYING AND SEEING)

Ask, You Have Nothing to Lose

Ask the devil in me the time, he'll tell
of a hanged human's pendulum antics in
"the only clockwork that counts."

Ask an angel, a rare visitor,
who'll answer: "Death's the alarm
each sleeper needs to catch a flight home,
and births are the notes he leaves for friends
too late to see him off."

The man who quotes the two so truly great's so awed,
he cannot choose not to speak

Words Concerned with Words

Hearing our nation's politicians' words,
I think of Miklos Radnoti, blessed
by a wife, who endured the horror and grief
Nazis had left her, and, from
a coat's decomposing pocket, saved
the years of love in her husband's words.

I think of Bridges and Brod, who broke their words
to Hopkins and Kafka and did not burn,
as their dying friends had asked,
lifetimes of words.

I think of we millions misled by words
of leaders who lead by pretending to save
us from whatever they've led us to fear,
and I am thankful for the fidelity of a wife
and for the betrayals of faithful friends, who saved
loving and deathless, words.

Student, Writing

Your writing said that you could ride a horse;
words pitching you headfirst till you seemed all dust,
but, learning to give least head with loosest rein,
you kept your saddle. And from your riding well
I know a sky rising from flatness, cattle red
on green, grown amid surrounding brown.

Seen in the careful opening of a door, your mom.

Your dad? His hand was as hard
as a hitching-post. His voice?
Hard, too. It was a fire-break, bared to protect a home,
a home whose artesian spring
surged out of split rock and sought to rise
as high as the ice of a peak, its source,
but fell and was dammed, and, about to try
writing as you had ridden, you fill
your canteen, from depths,
across whose surface a horse,
a boy, a man still move.

For a Former Mountain Climber

Eyes spring tarns seeking a way to sea,
he tells me words
must be what he's lived, or,
ink ice, he'll quit.

He was an Englishman in Afghanistan,
guiding imperialist tourists past
Muslims too long oppressed.
One flinch and he'd be,
for vermin, squirming among stones,
to escape his shadow, meat.
"I'm here," he says, "still here," and, yet,
in what should have been an ascent
as effortless as getting to one's feet after sleep,
in peaceful Switzerland,
he'd fought to stay, secure, on a ledge.

Roped down mountain, he'd never endanger another friend,
and, climber's calks chucked,
his alpenstock become a pen,
he leaves, syllable on syllable, a cairn of air
for survivors of other heights,
to warn of an avalanche in one.

Ecology, Biology and Poetry at Dawn

A big, bloody meatball, which will,
we pray, continue to feed us all,
begins to simmer on the horizon.

I've swept, off my picnic table, some spheres of what
a squirrel's digestion *could not*—
but that earth will be *able to*—use.

And, in a sky as luminous as this computer-screen, crows
dispute breakfast, then hurtle on,
on an alphabet's black, centuries-in-hatching, pinions,
until they fall or falter through thinner and thinner air
forever upward, to disappear
somewhere beyond all shadows' blazing source.

Meanwhile, question-mark curl of tail
balancing faith
in some perception of time and space
utterly beyond human perceptivity,
a squirrel leaps
from my cherry tree's crimson abundance, having left me
to write what it—gut stuffed with fruit, not ever to sprout
except in the orchard rows of poetry—could do without.

A Fancy Dancer, Ascending Among Mountain Flowers

(For the Pygmy Mammoths of Wrangle Island, for all of the women I have loved, from afar, or near, for Mary Ann Moore, who knew to rhapsodise, and, in memory of my father, whose Cherokee-Shawnee stomp dancing would shake, and shape, my world.)

I am dancing to bees' zither rhythms, and, with
their gracious or drunkenly heedless permission,
am dancing with the scent
of centuries of millions of beautiful women with
each breath each step
through blossoms toward clouds
imperceptibly thins.

Without missing a molecule of more
and more ethereal air,
I'm dancing with timberline pines, which shrink, degree
by chilling degree, cone after generation of cone,
their sweet, sun after sun, season on season, growth,
as Pygmy Mammoths, my fellow mammals, gene
on gene, grew smaller, to survive,
as has, century after century, word
after compressed word, our poetry.

Particles of mineral syllables beneath
each foot's sole's eloquent cells,
I am dancing, with giddy expectation, on
stone only glaciers have carved, when,
out of some utterly beyond me lexicon,
dawn wind, a fancy dancer, from every tribe,
whirls petals faster than any man,
thought by exuberant thought jigging, toward summit and
exhaustion's rhapsodic anticipation of fulfillment, can.

"Season of Mists and Mellow Fruitfulness"

(For John Keats and for Aristide Maillol)

No celebrations of colorful maples, staunch oaks,
and fall's tall cathedral-candles, dubbed ash.

With war in Iraq giving back to earth
metals and lovers' bodies, coupled with those
of animals turned, aeons ago, into oil,
one barely mentions bright leaves' prolongation
of blossoms' evocations
of sundowns and dawns.

Eloquent syllables dandelion futures blown
onto brown lawns, and, our world doomed
in military terminology
and science's phraseology,
this may be a time for sculpture timelessness,
minerals of chisels transforming minerals of stone
into seemingly enduring human forms.

From its propinquity to doomed-
to-disappear glaciers, the air
of breath tongue shapes into words is as gray as hair,
which clouds, in wind, the vision of one
who would gratefully let a leaf's pirouette
or a swirling skirt
make him forget that—
earth drowned in birth-blood from sun—
this could be his last day.

In the New Museum the Ancients' Art as Catharsis Theory Proves True

The drive from tea,
to keep him awake, so long,
his kidneys so old,
the men's room so new,
and, after the miles of night,
so confusingly bright,
he rushes in in time,
his mind on art's timelessness,
and hastily aims at the first visible
urinal, the one in
a shoeshine to combed hair mirror.

Moment in Museum

Nude women younger than she,
or anyone alive ever was, the guard,
who stalks after a lone old man, seems
as resolute as a mother, to see
that he does not appreciate
the bodies of those who posed,
instead of their spiritual beauty, and he—

a lover, yes, but only of art,
a lawyer might plead before God—

attempts to seem as pious as Christ,
in a niche, adjacent to the women's room's
opening and closing door.

His prayer is that his inquisitor
will leave him be,

To be or not to be? the question posed,
each moment before, or after, closing-time,
by every sculpture here.

Adam and Eve, Freiburg Modern Art Museum

The size of whatever wood was there to be carved,
the woman and man are proportioned like pit ponies, small
for mine tunnels but strong
for hauling coal, which will fuel the industry
of an expanding Christianity.

Doomed to live and die
on a tiny, ice-bound island,
mammoths mated to shrink,
baby by baby, for generations, to survive
on minimal food as long as they could.

My enormous nation hunts—
a Second Coming, a Second Going—animal fossils'
megatons of metamorphosed browse, reborn
as molecules of oil, but one
descendant of Eve and Adam carved
centuries of trees' growth to fit upon
the mantel of a human living room.

The Calm of Bronze

Bronze uniform as bright
as the jacket of a bullet
among leaves as vulnerable as breaths,
the statue was cast
to outlast a young man's flesh,
whose comely chemistry a young woman,
her children unborn, her beautiful cells
a century among struggling roots, could,
as can we, only mourn.

Photo of Neighboring Farm Couple

Disinclined to fight, his only scars
are the ones sixty some years of harvests
inflicted on his hands.

His wife—
so *his* he needs a stranger's camera to see
her sturdy, enduring beauty—
appreciates
his body's being as straight as the handle of his hoe,
where hers perpetuates memories of valleys and hills,
whose grains her oven immortalizes.

Their sons ambitious for glory and gone
into military cemeteries,
loaf after loaf, her half of the bed still pledges his.

Renoir's Couples Dancing, We, Depending on Which Century, Kiss or Do Not

My sweetheart mine,
yours yours, we are in
cyclonic tuxedos
and skirts' swirling surf,
surrounding as song does, and, yes,
as air does—the air
of breathing and panting and sighing and weeping and words
—
and we are dancing a long-ago dance,
cheeks to our—flesh, then—cheeks, and, yes,
as tongue's ardent thrumming does, as
that seemingly merely accompanying drum, the heart, does,
canvas and pigment, save
some minuscule mementoes of loves we live.

Homage to Henry Moore's Sculptures on an Outer Wall of the Römer Cathedral, Frankfurt am Main, and the Figures of Christ Inside

(for Philip McCracken, sculptor, and for Michael Wüstefeld, poet)

Risen for good, a crucified Child smiles,

   and smiled while emperors,
   heads bent beneath gems embedded in gold, strained
   to rise from brocade-encumbered knees.

Moore's essences,

   as faceless as foetuses, kings formed from,
   and financiers and bombardiers

redeem all

   this side of this wall
   of this cathedral, which rises,
its shadow placental, reborn
from bomb-blasted rubble,
   each stone a fit like the click of a clock.

A Sublime Matisse Odalisque and a U.S. Grotesque

Her torso twisting out
of pajama pants' seashell stripes,
the odalisque's armpit's evocative of
a less accessible niche,
each nipple's a point to be taken
in caliph's counsel soon
to be convened, and,
so big they're about to burst like birthday balloons,
the couch's upholstering's blossoms belong
among Eden's megatons of dinosaur browse
which aeons compressed into fuel the West
immolates Middle East millions to burn.

Still Life, Museum Living Room

The telephone is garroting itself,
trying to splice or to twist in two in time
a wire which might have borne
preliminaries for treaties or war declarations'
great weight, or the thousands
of generations of infant cries
smothered in one lover's goodby.

Over a crucifix, a slave-days clock—
its black, its white, its gold—

And, Brother, Sister, maybe opening for me, or for you,
who may stumble through rubble this place will surely be,
in time—or *out*—a door,
familiar fingerprints, on knob and, in oak grain,
the whorls of the print of an Unimaginable Hand.

Celebrity and Nail

(Young woman, flustered, having seen me on page one,
"I'm sorry. I know you're a celebrity, but I can't remember
your name."—as I ask for my hospital bill.)

You enter a room,

shoe-sole-nail a cat's claw
at fraying carpet,

and everyone stands,

silk dresses caressing breasts in the moment of ascension,
neckties an Eden of cobras writhing in rising—

your fans, in their best, honoring you,

who have traveled too far, too long,
to get here's the fact,
no matter what headlines say,

and there wasn't any river, despite
a map's blue worm's wriggling's being given your name,

no war, though the thousands you sacrificed won it, and,

no frescoes, fading from cathedral-rubble walls,
while scholars discover more than anyone could,
in a lifetime, have done.

Toes worrying threads
you would save everyone
from tiring toward tripping upon,
you softly say, sincerely,

"I am extremely fatigued—"
to thunderous applause, for they knew,
always, your dream
would come true and fulfill their,
impossible, own.

"Just bushed, wasted–exhausted, goddammit!
Just really beat to shit."

But already, shyly, the youngest in the room
is dreaming of wearing soles free from nails.

SECTION TWO

(WAR: DECLARATIONS, EVOCATIONS AND CONDEMNATION)

"It was as if an entire nation had decided to commit suicide."

U.S. diplomat held hostage by Iranians.

Sheep Ranch Home, Near Air Base

(For Doe Tabor and Kristy Athens)

Blade-winged bombers shearing blue pastures' white
fleece, a flower-garden's fence, wool tufts caught on it,
could seem Grandmother's loom,
Cherokee-Shawnee forebears—dragooned
from homes, midwinter—clothed
in warm air lovingly woven by her tongue.

Wire rusts, and, just as
we authors do, until applause dies,
decomposing posts bow, their doom
to remain in earth, a time,
sustaining, maybe, a tree's burgeoning.

Some words, said or read, send planes
through oxygen-poor stratosphere. Some words could fence
animals' teeth from petals and
grandchildren's children's children from harm.

Warplanes, Hummingbird, Cat and Poet

Its beak deep in Christmas-hibiscus-dyed drink,
centering a view-window's snow,
the hummingbird, a blaze on its breast,
has frozen my cat and me,

the cat tensed to pounce
against glass, as clear
as the air words share with wings
of warplanes, bearing minerals meant to wilt,

my intent to seem
as lifeless as my body will surely, one day, be
and let a trigger-finger-sized creature feel safe to feed
from plastic petals, flared
like exploded bomb,
or breast feathers' blossoming dawn.

Blossoms, Wings, Words

An airplane writing “bird” on “rain”in my brain
and “bloom” a word, as is “bomb,”
the shape of a tooth cratering my fist,
from learning to fight, while learning to write, in school,
I could stay silent if not afraid of losing my only chance
at delaying what may tear air
of unspoken prayers from lungs,
tear brick from brick
and flesh from flesh, while
a hummingbird—travel its only hope of survival—beaks
nectar, to fuel the flutters, from here
to where it will winter,
each sip, each syllable, more crucial as final petals fall

Descendants, an All-But-Extinct Bird's and an Almost-Vanished Vanishing American's

Trees hacked down decades ago,
and nailed into subdivision rows,
wings crash against glass,
then fly away,
to nest, perhaps, in the shade
of an anachronism
and leaving, as shuddering reflection,
an Indian hunter
startled he's alive's great
great grandson's
pale ghost.

Night Sky, Indian Ridge

This sky,
at which my eyes will stare,
as empty as it,
is as black as the aeons of life
compressed by the weight of earth and sea
and transformed to fuel for car,
to plastic for steering-wheel,
to highway tar. A war,
for more and more, transforming thousands of tons
of flesh, my wife and I, driven by love, drive, down,
from an infinity of ice and peace and join
children and grandchildren, in
our, nuclear-target, home.

Going Home, After Camping on Indian Ridge

Their orbits ancestors' campfire rings,
our stars, which time or timelessness ignited,
become, because we need them to be,
bright lights of other commuters.

My Country Again Threatening Aggression

(This time, for oil in Iraq.)

The sea, though equally lethal, killing millions, seems sane,
as it destroys our own and nations we call enemies.

More mathematically predictable than Christians, our
crusaders will change ocean to oil
then celebrate, not in cathedral
or temple or mosque but in banks,
the union of women and men—
and children—with earth,
not sensing for even one instant
the sea's awesome aeons of giving and taking away.

A Killer Seeking Forgiveness

From where I will kill
a fellow creature, as
my Indian people have,
for generations, done,

I see
a porcupine,
its waddling body an ambulatory cactus,
which only the most benign intentions
of a poet's tongue would even try to ease
into garden row or vase—

see pines,
which fought, like two of too many children,
for each other's ration of sun,
and, now, the stronger lives on,
to gloat or to grieve—

and see,
disputing snow crimsoned by
some earlier hunter's good fortune, crows,
as black as oil spilled by temblor
or greed's heedlessness or war.

A sentinel crow is able to see, not me
but camouflaging leaves, from trees,
whose wood may heat someone's home
and cook someone's food eventually,

and, then, while wind weaves vines,
as if to mitten this trigger-finger hand,

my desperate family's first meat,
after days of hunger, comes,
browsing some blossoms so
forgiving they are still enduring this freezing fall.

A Hunt and After

Mountain storms feared
or more deer lower,
we should not climb, he tried
to persuade, but our adolescent insults drove him—
as stones, thrown, drive game into bullets—
higher, until his dread
of heights hit harder than our words,
and we had to guide our numbed friend down,
to where it was only racists' knives,
and, next year, war he,
and we, had to fear.

A Survivor of the Depression and World War Two, I Read a Daily Paper

For most of us alive
in 21st Century USA, story means news,
but Mom and Dad's first child dead
from hunger and sickness, I find nothing new
about children's being fed
to earth. Not pity but boredom
is maybe what we should be sharing,
given the similarity
of wars, throughout history, but,
my parents sacrificing their own
dwindling strength to feed
the already stunted growth of each child,
I have lived to give my children
grim warnings and
glimpses of petals' sometimes successful attempts
at redemption of rubble and
whatever else has grown from my parents' love.

Some Future Soldiers' Tic-Tac Attack

(Tic-Tacs are homemade noisemakers.)

Spools emptied of thread
in patching our pants, we notched rims
to look like gears grinding tanks
over dads' stories' enemies.

Then, tight-wound string yanked, Tic-Tacs spun
around pencil axles, and, held
against a meeting room's glass, they made
such a disrespectful noise grown men
played hooky from choosing one friend's daughter or
a prettier for our teacher next year and—
war-whooping movie Indians—chased
their triumphant futures, vanishing as fast as their pasts.

Becoming a Man, World War Two

My father running the oat-stalk-slashing threshing-machine,
my older brother planting Nazis in newsprint rows,
fifteen, and doing our family's share
of neighborhood work,
I'd hear grown men say to me,
at the end of the day,
"You're pretty damned smart,"
impressed that an Indian,
just past puberty, could tell by the sun
the same hour watches said.

My, and their daughters', thighs
our nation's next generation's V's
for Victory, steeple bells' history
of ultimate defeat chimed
and told the time.

Sky Bent

(for Aunt Jenny, my other mother)

The boy whose trigger finger corked a dike,
thumb up, as if to hitch hike to the U.S.—"What—"
my Aunt Jenny would say—"What a tyke!"

And on the burning deck
of a ship those in the know
were fleeing, as rats would soon flee from
Hiroshima and an electrified grill
in Psychology 101, a loyal lad,
obeying the gentleman who'd sired him, waited—
despite the urging of some
less upright citizens—where commanded to wait.

A mixed-breed, mixed up Native American boy
who'd learned Colonial England's moral tales
in rhyme in his more realistic time, I startled awake,
my German-American half-brother yelling, "Oh, Hell!"
and bounding downstairs
to rouse Mom and Dad,
our window glowing like movie neon,
the barn the butt
of a harvest hand's cigarette so huge
it might have been a rocket except
no buzz-bombs were over London yet.

Among men as excited as kids at Halloween,
I ran, shoeless, though that was not allowed
because of the possibility of injury's
resulting in an infection and
a doctor bill we could not afford
or lockjaw, which
had killed a distant relative

though somebody busted out teeth
and poured soup, through a funnel, down.

Barefoot on grass, cropped short as a soldier's hair,
or life; on drive-way-gravel sharp

as cartoon-fakirs' nail-studded beds;
and on squishy chicken-shit;
I leaped like a ballet-dancer I
would not see for twenty some years
and would—if I had—have considered him "a fruit,"
which I'd not heard about yet.
Swatting at mossy shingles gliding like bats
with their fur on fire, I yelled,
startling neighbors' disapproval awake, "Oh, hell!"
the Christian version of what I was
enjoying, a church bell summoning
the fire-fighter volunteers,
Dad paid yearly dues to, too late,
my Sunday school rebel's splendor-loving soul caught
in a sky-bent, cathedral-tall blaze.

A Bomber Crewman's Dance Around the Dead

I didn't like steel, and the animosity
between aeons-old minerals
and my 18-year-old self
was seemingly mutual.

As I dangled from a catwalk two miles
of freezing air above peaks' polar bear teeth,
these hands—which had devoted time
to prayer, but more
to the mystery of girls'
impossible to divine futures—were battered by jammed
shackle and bomb, steel's way of asking, why,
if it could instantly kill eight,
including me, should it consent to wait
until it fell and imitated volcanos' incinerating hundreds?

A safety wire—a copper-cobra , writhing in bomb bay wind—
persuaded back into its den in a fuse,
explosion remained in hibernation, and, when I forced
the bomb casing's ring
to fit the bomb-rack's bent finger, bomb
and bomber were joined in an unholy matrimony,
not to be put asunder, until
divorce would tell
a story, with no ending.

Bird, Cat and Soldier, Between Battles

Bayonets thrust into earth,
rifle rows parody parade,
and sling-buckles click
dirges against trigger-guards in wind,
which stirs survivors from timelier planting, platoons of corn,
stalks' brown the brown of uniforms—on one,
as bright as a battle-ribbon, a bird,
which would have to tunnel warm
and warmer air, infinitesimal times greater than
the volume of its tiny lungs, to find—
beyond the stretching of generations of poets' tongues—
a tropical foliage, for camouflage.

And you can but murmur, "Beauty," before,
your orders loud and clear,
thought slits into that of a cat,
whose gunsight-eyes see splendor as appetite.

Old German Woman, Some Wars

"Help me!" she cries, faltering, reckless or trusting, from tram,
a survivor of bombs, most likely, and, now,
a flesh-and-blood bomb herself,
the only possible target, me.

I'm old, she's older, and I've no time to accuse,
"Coventry's rubble," or her, the name
of a map-coordinate I'd flown to set aflame.

Her hand finds the hand I've offered, her feet meet
the cobblestoned earth, we share
with thousands of the living and with
those billions, who waltz, in petal gowns,
or, snail-shell-helmeted, march,

her thanks an echo of mine,
war ending, my bomber turning away from this city,
my fate to live to write to be
ignored, or read, by all
I would love to save.

A Cherokee Airman Remembers Two Wars

His Cherokee people's blood,
a century thinned by the Mississippi,
below his rowboat's prow, recalls
a river curled, brown
like an English gallows' rope
around Laotian huts, as small
as those he'd raised
from his father's bad luck poker deck and wrecked,
and wrecked again, under the moment's shade bombs made
on whatever game Laotian children played.

A Cherokee Secular Formula to Cure Egoism

Your house, car, prick, wife's breasts
too big for Christian humility—
the post-World-Wars-One-and-Two-
and-so-on male American problem—try

imagining yourself an astronaut,
even your humblest bodily functions
requiring meticulous care
in order for you not to meet
yesterday's admirably-balanced diet's
rejectamenta adrift in orbit.

Space Station become
a, golden, diaper-delivery van,
your after-taxes wages still
not small enough, think
that the planets were excreted from the Sun
and one of them grew
the flowers whose petals your family will strew
like vivid subway stubs,
the underground traveler you.

An American, in a Polyester Suit, on an Egyptian Beach

In plastic pants,
derived from plants,
which megatons of earth pressed
into petroleum, he bares
his vision of skins.

Black is a nightmare,
a hangover won't let
him forget.

Yellow's the color of—
nose indicates the Gents.

Brown? Swaddling the wrinkles of his frown around
his sunburned daughter's Bikini, he

sees red
as an affront to his bluecoat great-
great-grandad—taxes better spent
to nuke the surviving savages, no reservations.

Indian complexion paled
when England's rapists sailed, I smile on
the next generation's
darkening skin's Go to hell rebellion
and compliment
the fossil-source suit
the world will bury her sire in.

A Meditation on Aging

Where he was once in love
with the prettiest illusion in the room,
he's become a spectator,
to feminine skin, extensively visible between
the motherly intentions of minimal cloth.

He's become a reader of philosophical-spiritual tomes,
mild How to Do It manuals for
a hopeful aspirant to heaven, and, his mind
like earth's dried crust, his thoughts
are petals he's dropped on family graves
dust soon to be thrown—like clods he threw
to hasten horses through a gate—on his own.

Peaches in the Pantry,
Some Rhymes for Smug Inheritors

Once was an Indian,
        you know it was so,
                killed for his river land,
                        his tombstone snow.

Once was a forest. Yes,
        but these days.
                you nail it into subdivisions thank-
ing Jesus Mary Loving God for
        ancestors' greediness, their
                musketry, your nuclear bombs
and undeserved luck,
        peaches in the pantry
                pleasantness in bed
Vanishing Americans
        buried in your head—but
                trying to rise
                        trying to be free
even as this Indian
        yes it is so
                harvests family memories,
                        snow letters carved in snow.

A Nightmare After 9-11

(For Jeff, Brian and Martina)

Shore's hordes of breakers not quite awakening me,
I defied a mob, maybe the one I actually
escaped–their tar, feathers and knife.

Vanishing Americans vanished again,
flesh they bequeathed me fleeing and buying a gun,
with which, My Children,
I later turned back attack,
and you could be born.
What's more enduring than nightmare,
and stronger than memory,
is moon's persuading tides aeons before
Columbus' invasion and engendering poetry
centuries before imperialism's wronged
turned planes, and themselves, into bombs.

Boat Song

The edge of the boat—

no time to try
to learn "gunwale" and be somebody else—

the edge of all you have tried to live and say,

some integers of war,
some moments of love,
the consequences of,

the next generation, the air
their words will shape, the air
that they will take,
as you have done,
overboard or on,
in life vest or lungs.

SECTION THREE

(CENTURIES OF LOVERS)

A Junior High Glimpse of the Future

A girl bends to tie her shoe,
and fall wind elevates
her skirt, as blue
as a morning glory blossom, blamed,
in the Literature hour, for centuries of poetry's
symbolic lechery.

Pistil and stamen yet to be learned, a boy
responds, with an eloquent nothing, to
the future's accusatory stare. The only way
he can hold his own is to, finally,
reluctantly say,
"Oh, pardon me
for living," a sarcasm engendered, perhaps, by war,
and older schoolmates absent from here
where soon to wilt petals flaunt
glory and prim, woven cotton inches ascend.

Love Story with Inevitable Denouement

Maybe in love, let's say,
and certainly fervently into adventurous sex,
in exhilarating surroundings, he knelt,
the river so cold it wilted erection, and kissed
or missed and only briefly slightly warmed
her not surprisingly goose-bump-roughened thigh.

Their shared fear of breath's
endearments becoming final bubbles not
an occasion for orgasms, multiple or single,
with no afterglow reflections on life-
destroying glacier and life-
engendering sea, he and she, emerge hastily
from surges a celestial beauty urges toward neap
or a more prosaic tide, then join, for a time,
like adjacent grains of sand
in television's warm and soft
and comforting strand,
and marry and start a family,
to be done in by common mortality,
or, too many having voted stupidly,
to be obliterated precipitously by bombs.

Bird Heard, Leopards, Sloths and Lovers Glimpsed

Bird cry or come cry startling me awake,
my eyes climb sheer flights of air
to the city's maybe only two lights
beyond my solitary, second-story own.

Yesterday's university students, I guess,
books holding bodies back
from battering together in human imitation of
an arboreal feline mating frenzy, become,
after an inevitable culmination,
the seemingly infinitely calm
whispering together of sloths.
But only in cerebration. In art
two perfectly in time timeless darknesses no words can douse
explode, as blinding as sunrise after sunrise or
New Years or Christmas or
Independence Night rockets in your and my
unknown, unknowable, future lovers' eyes.

A Time in the Zoo

Quite colorful, the backthrust butt
of an orangutan in heat's
a monster flower, missing its stalk.

The centuries of romantic poetry
are useless to me, in love recently, for the first time,
and, 60 years later, a grandfather, for the third.

A bomber, not one of the ones I flew in
in World War Two, but probably nuclear, above,

A small hand in foetal curl inside my hand,
"What they doing?" to answer,

Saving the world's, my thought,
while ancestors gambol in my brain,

"Just having fun," my words.

Centuries of Lovers

Where finger and thumb gripped
wet newsprint hard in wind,

among today's "Casualties,"
are ink prints a poet understands
as love notes centuries of lovers wrote,

those prints more yours than parental worry-wrinkles
in mirror or words, and you—

a veteran of war
after war, yours or your lover's or child's,
or grandparent's, or great's
or greatgreat's—or
you're only a somewhat concerned
newspaper-reader.

A poet might have left it at that
but for harder wind.

Remembering Innocence

(i.)

"And, so, you go with an Indian soldier," her brother said,
his generations of Spanish pride
offended by my girlfriend's shy acquiescence to
whatever future she and I—
quite glamorously uniformed,
and paled by generations-ago coupling, but
discernibly non-
Caucasian—might find.

"I guess you must really love me,"
she whispered to herself,
to my urgent lips,
to the film lovers we
could still believe we might become,
not yet having heard what her family
and the army had to say.

(ii.)

Some kissing on the TV
I gave my family after the war,
"I guess they must really love one another,"
was all my, embarrassed, mother's sister could think,
her love life one date,
according to girlishly persistent teasing.

Though elderly, I bare, reluctantly,
while swimming, the handsbreadth scar
a surgeon left in closing the arched door
to my repaired heart, and,
two memories handholds on a wishbone, I pray
that my children's children's children may live beautifully.

Dawn Coffee Stop, Nearing Home

Hours of highway, as empty as my thermos, led
to a glass pot of coffee so black
it could be night sky,
its boiling's bubbles meteors,
returning to invisibility,
as syllables will when my tongue
heats air no more.

And years and years led
to a hand, which pours
alacrity I'll need, from here to home,
and raises, lover after lover, from beds
of others, and, from her grave,
Mother, then rises, itself—
sun risen in skin as evanescent as cloud—in farewell.

A Grandfather's Hope, Wish or Prayer

This instant of this calendar year
as inconsequentially small, in inconceivable Time,
as our earth, in our universe,
thin clouds are reminders that whites of eggs
were sustenance for meat-tearing teeth of reptiles, some
to mutate into birds,
whose songs share air
with poetry, and bombs.

Three children, two grandchildren and a third
soon to be born, and to be gone,
beyond metaphor's woven-together feathers and twigs,
pale shards of shell, as blue as snow clouds
leave sky, will tell
of robins' survival, and will recall
that lifetimes of suns,
as yellow as yolks, still feed
whatever is destined to fledge and fly
and sing and die.

Early Planting

Among toy military vehicles,
whose colors are those of the fall,
and kits for little nurses, I buy this spring's seeds,
my mother alive in her cautioning not
to scatter too many and risk,
in this year's planting, all
that she'd carefully chosen from the last.

Hunger, sickness and wars survived,
I tear one corner off one packet and, my nation again
squandering young women and men
on unnecessary plunder, I space seeds and words,
and pray, like generations before me, for rain.

A Glimpse Between the Pool Hall's Blinds

Her nakedness as white as my winter breath
in Main Street's only late night window's light, a girl,
against whose butt I'd bounced
a rubber ball tethered with a rubberized string
during operetta practice, was spread on the green
felt of a table, where I had won
at Rotation and Crazy Eight,
less often than I'd lost.

Balls bulges in pockets, cue-sticks racked,
the name of the game was beer,
for sure, and maybe whisky, and men
older than I'd ever be,
lined up, like first graders for the teeter-totter, to play.

For My Wife's Father, Edward Wendt

This view-home's sundown side's whole wall
a window as clear as a waterfall,
glistens of coffins sliding like kids' sleds down
a street, wrenched steep by earthquake, were what memory made
my wife's father make
of our valley's other side's lights'
glacier glitters, and, though I know
that turbine tornados herd melted snow's stampede-flow
into a lamp's tungsten's blind canyon, the lightning strike
which I survived when I was a kid illuminates
this page, on which I write, that
the man who fathered the mother of my daughter slides,
tonight, down words wrenched crooked
as buried years and lives collide.

An American-Indian Success Story in India

My abandoned grandmother's raising twelve kids—
two years of study all that my father could get,
before racism shut down his school—
six years of university for me, after what
the army had taught—

a Bombay newspaper reporter—
to whom I'd given an interview
after her union's strike had ended
press-censorship—honored my family
as a Native American success story.

Although assaulted in their legislature,
India Indian women won freedom for everyone,
and I would honor here those
who honored my American Indian father and grandmother.

SECTION FOUR

(SOME FORESHADOWINGS)

A Defense Against the Evil Without and the Evil Within

Moments ago, in the dark,
the lock to my hotel room
clicked, and I sprang from bed, this hand,

(again armed with pen)
a fist, when,
fleeing feet left
a door ajar, and left

my body, nerves charged
for murder, to be caught
in the cracks and clear
condemnation of an old mirror.

Two Poems in Memory of Nils-Aslak Valkeapää (B. 1943, D. 2001)

(i.)

Wolf-Kill, from Turi's *Book of Lapland*

(remembering the Chernobyl disaster year, when Nils-Aslak and I first exchanged poems)

Skis swift boats over ocean-waves'
evaporation's frozen precipitation

which breaks
as drifts, and slows
paws,

pole,

shaped to scrape snow off browse,

useless as weapon this close,

you
jam hand into growl,

enduring fangs
jagged as ice-edge in storm-surf
slaver,

and choke gullet,

until a last gasp contorts,
onto generations
of tongues:

an ancestor's, ineffectual, bludgeon swung,
 and an arm plunged
 between teeth,

while Chernobyl's invisible packs,
 ravage descendants'
  deer.

(ii.)

I Learn of the Death of a Friend,

and tundra swans are snow
blown over miles and miles
of the sunlit wings
of Skagit Valley daffodils.

Ochoco Forest, a Sound in the Night

Breath between teeth flared
to speak or to bite,
an exhortation to Belief or to war,

the cry of, maybe, a bear,

or of the centuries
of trees, now cities,

or of Earth's last plea, lost
on industry's insanity's bombardiers—

the baying of hounds, and a distant shot
are as near as I've come, to knowing what
what waked me might have been.

Grateful

Like a grounded whale,
lungs crushed, without water to buoy
a slow avalanche of meat, Jesus died,
as any of us would, if crucified,
from muscles' sagging's causing suffocation,
avers a man whose life
study's the *Bible*.

Like an army ant
nuzzling another for chemicals essential to live,
I beg what I need
to know to shape words you,
Reader, may need,
to send, into our ocean of air,
your own great grateful spume,
of whatever breath descent into depth
has left you—a contribution
to inflation for more comfortable automobile travel or
to fragrances of funeral and wedding bouquets.

To My Heart, an Emancipation Proclamation

"Art is the ax to break the frozen sea within us."
Franz Kafka

Old Slave, blind pumper at the well,
one brother already dead,
you kept me alive,
through hunger and fever, to chop ice
and save cattle from thirst.

Their milk sustaining my, and, thus,
my children's children's destinies,
no wonder if, after all of these years,
you threaten the ultimate revolt,
and I can only say, gratefully, that—
known truly by those understanding your urge to be
the fertility-dance drum-beat of poetry—
you endure, so far,
as does, despite stupidity
and greed, our world.

Inner Page

They are young again, old friends,
in photos survivors have chosen,
grins' rows as uniform as ranks
of soldiers we all once were—

the hours of terror,
exhaust fumes of bombers, or parked cars'
minutes of breath-mints and ears,
as fragrant as petals, eager to hear
a promise only that
bachelor bastard Hitler or
our own bachelor habits could break,
dim lights uniting shadows, so slender, then,
gone into once and for all,
inner-page obituary words—

on television screens,
our leaders repeating
the glorious stories of nations which once had been.

Medical Advice, from a Patient

Don't even try to make friends with death.

You can grin your best grin,
for the receptionist,
flirt with the nurse, and
flatter the doctor,
delaying even longer his schedule for
delivering bad news, but
you are just as well off telling death off,
right at the start,
in delivery room or connubial bedroom,
yelling at sky, Oh, my
Heavens!— my
God!—my
word!—
knowing full well or
as sure as hell or
whatever else rhymes,
that nothing, not
one damned thing,
in this whole, holy world, is yours.

The Eloquent Bones, a Second Coming

Christ comes back from death, and there
could be a life of love for which to prepare,
and, yet, your dog raises a leg
above an azalea's noon blaze
as if to extinguish humanity's last chance at beauty,
and somebody, interested in oil, raises an army,
and something you might have lived
presses finger prints' arabesque snakes onto door knobs,
our identity the eloquent bones we leave in graves.

Hospital Parking Lot

Chrome sparkling in sun,
like rows of devotional candle flames,
I think of women and men awaiting directions
from those whose care
is not the destination but the means of getting there, all
those miles, from zero to zero,
from birth to death, all
of those unknown, unknowable miles,
and bodies—one of them mine—
my car to be, at the end
of the day, driven home or elsewhere.

Every Damned One

His wife had seen a deer,
the first living one since the Indians,

in the garden of this showplace house
constructed with stone

which sea creatures formed when life
jiggled and glistened like gysm on a thigh

until aggressive enough to gain
the shore and grab
a steering wheel, its plastic derived from
the same petroleum exploded
in faster cars and jets like shooting stars
compared to his plane nicknamed "Flying Coffin" in
the war he had won—
all that a man once lived for, his son,
gone, like so many, in the tin,
titanium and rubber war, the U.S. lost—and, when
deer ate the little woman's blossoms, every damned one,
his helpmeet for twenty eight, give
or take, years, could only say,
tears silver wires stitching cheeks, "I wish one had come
when our child was young."

Night Highway, War

Half of a whisky flask in my head,
the night ice, the distance to home hours,
I am a hitchhiker, needed to drive
because the owner of the car,
a pilot older than me by three war years, needs sleep.

Ten men dead, today,
their bomber burning in my brain,
and more than he can count
the combat veteran's weeks
of not counting on anything—
a headlight ahead I wake and veer
in time, and in time the war will end
and some of us will live and need
to sometimes mention, as new wars start,
memories of friends.

Three Visitations or Evocations

(For Joe "Dog"Smith)

(i)

Old friend and fellow Cherokee,
my aches, exhaustion, years and memories
at rest in the chair in which you died,

it was good to have you back,

even as a Stellar's Jay's
swift flight past glass, through which
you must have seen the sun the pines
were storing, to see them through until spring,
fade.

(ii)

"A spirit come back as a duck?"
a skeptic teacher, decades dead, scoffs,
so emphatically graves' blossoms jump,
like the kindergartners all teachers once were,
out of their fidgeting rows.

"Come back?"
Not ever really gone, my friend,
a long time—and, now—*now*—
timelessly—grown
wise in the ways of grown-ups, replies,
politely, "Quack. QuackQuack. Quack!"

(iii)

A deer, the day of your death, appears,
near the end of my yard and stares,
for an hour, or more, my way; then,
as I move to find a pen,
whose ink will dry
on combustible paper—
or vanish, as we Cherokees are said
to be doing—in air, the air of Whites' words—you ascend
the slope to my apple tree,
a spirit, yes, in my mind and in my yard, and, yet, a deer,
a tranquil deer—at home, in our world
and the next—well fed and ready for winter.

The Suicide of the Son of a Friend

There is war across the Adriatic, the Balkans again,
and there are too many tons
of bodies beneath centuries of stone for my
compassion to try to fly
the Atlantic, home, but too much grief
in my life not to feel
the bullet in the brain of my friend's son,
inflicting some sense of some coming destruction, my own.

Some Last Words for a Young Poet

Whatever I'd say too late
to help her weakening hand,
to turn the gas off or the clock back,
to whatever needed to be changed,

I could say of her:

A life of beauty, pain spared,

but what I must say

is that no one can say
what she would have said
and has, in a way—
her way—continued to say.

For Don Monroe

A blue heron flew into our drainage-ditch.
the day Don left the rest of us
to find that his mind—which had spanned
our entire land—had mapped an emptiness
pills could not fill.

I remember thinking my dad,
who'd killed to save his life,
defiant of death,
my mother telling me "No,
at the last, he cried like a child."

And, as I mourn, I, who have had to write
terror, despair and love
to stay alive, labor, to give
my children mouthfuls of air,
with enough density to bear
a descendant of aeons of awesome wings, to nest in
the tangled tendrils of a human brain.

Seven Days After Burying My Brother

It is important not to go deep,

a mouse sensing a snake,

a submarine with a damaged hatch,

a meteor blistering its belly on the air
of anyone's poem.

War on, One Brother, Sixteen, and, I, Fourteen, Try to Be Men

Hands numb on the bridled heads, of colts, when they bolt,
I'm jolted so hard I'm blinded, but blades
of the corn-stalk-cutting machine,
could slice me into bacon strips, I know,
and, though unconscious, I keep my grip on straps.

My brother, heels set, slight weight sliding through mud,
hauls back hard on the reins, his yell
more compelling than words
of gratitude I'd send, 68 years
late, through earth we labored to prepare
for planting one day we
and our soldier brother and all
alive, in the war-besotted world, shared.

A Zebra-Stripe Kite in Gray Sky Above Flags and Graves

Eleven, my Irish-American mother's first son—

who lost his German-American father in World War One
and lived, despite German bullets, through World War Two—

nailed apple-crate slats, to make a cross, and where
feet, hands and crown of thorns were,
in the picture at the top of our stair,
he tied string taut, to edge two skeletal wings,
stirred water and flour and glued
newspaper skin, whose black,
"DEPRESSION ... NEW DEAL ... ATOMIC WAR ... "
and white stripes of nothing between, fly
in memory, today, a century's flag, in implosion-torn sky,
above steel stems' red, white and blue petals,
which flourish, although snow falls
on coffins flown back
from sunshine in Iraq
for my brother's and for we younger survivors' salute.

Crossed crate-slats' slivers
wounding a future trigger-finger,
zebra-skin news
and dangling rag tail rose, and rise,
to spliced string's and thought's
ultimate reach,
spacecraft and Other Hopes too high to see.

For Robert Wessels

My half brother, whose German-American father died,
in the American army, in World War One, was,
in World War Two, captured by Germans, who
flew him from Tunisia to Sicily.

Escaped, he worked on farms,
for a hiding place and food,
while Italian sons were U.S. prisoners of war.

Pick grapes, scythe wheat—
make wine, bake bread,
a little sanity
among millions of the mad.

Two Birds, One Air Rifle BB and a Summer Without Rain

(i.)

The first hummingbird I'd ever seen,
its feathers as green as grass had been before
fields parched, fell dead a few wing beats short
of the livestock-drinking-tank,
whose windmill's shadow's a sun dial's count,
now touching my eightieth year.

(ii.)

After war after war after war,
after land, after gold, after oil,
my air rifle BB seems
inconsequential, but,
to one sparrow, gray breast become
the dawn or sunset a hummingbird bears
from birth to death, the copper sphere,
tinier than any conceivable egg, was
an asteroid collided with our world.

(iii.)

My thoughts, my best aimed thoughts,
nothing to those whose ink
sends commands to kill, one BB has swelled
into a cannon-shell, which
my soldier brother had to spade earth—
as tongue must delve air—the depth
of a grave to survive.

Rented Rooms, London, New York

Chair springs squeak, like my boyhood bedroom's mice,
and my ageing aching body's door
to a shower's my own ghost,
complaining that I did not die young.

These years, when there's more to write than to live,
I am, again, dancing on floors too new to creak,
beneath combat boots and slender slippers,
my fingers learning guns'
and women's mysteries—ahead,
as I remember a bomber's uncertain flight:
an unlighted landing-strip, or none.

A New Year's Fantasy, on Broadway

I'm elbowing among, when, out
of briefcases' secrecy,
a ticker-tape blizzard of war-
oratory melts
into poetry's cloudburst uncertainty.

Syllables lovers share, to fuse or confuse
the eternal with the splendidly temporary,
blossom, and falling petals spell,
on concrete's, reluctant to yield, ice,
My God! we are of the same species.

Gray-gowned by cold,
our tongues', teeth's, lips' emissaries warm
the nearest frostbitten ears. Good!
It feels so good! We love
one another's fun
and profundity. We love
the summers in one another's lungs.

Photograph of My Father as Van Gogh's Peasant in Straw Hat

Even in the blurriness
of the hasty documentary, the sun
shows corn as tall as any man
could demand of a season, or a son,

who—despite the afflictions
of poverty and war—
takes courage from seeing his own reflection,
in eyes, under winter horizons arched
as high as they can rise,
to hold, as much as possible, of all
that has so long sustained hope
in white's foreshadowings of green.

A Ritual for Approaching My Father's Death

A benign-intentioned gopher—bare-ground-brown
or green-striped to blend with grass? Don't ask.
No side-tunneling, timid of death.

My mind must keep straight on,

and burrow garden dirt glued
to fact's ghost-ocean-bed clay, then through
the best volcanoes could do
to equal astronauts' future ascents.

Passing the arrow-nicked bones
of soldiers and settlers and buffalo,
and Indians' cannon-shattered skeletons,

I climb from roots of oats,
a gopher no longer, where
the air of final words stirs
like a breeze bringing the chill of fall,
my father at work, and not singing, as his poet son
would have him do, the old songs, no,
but asking a caller, as I ask Death, to wait
until a wagon accumulating harvest is full.

A Ceremony for Trying to Accept Death

One tries to tell a truth about death, which will reassure all:

first, frogs fighting last blizzard's roar for
their generation's share of air
to shape into hope in ears;

then, petals—which fell, among maple-leaves'
encouragingly slow-to-fade blaze, on graves—now risen, in
time
for weddings, joining in the centuries of processes'
assimilation into sun's small family circle.

One senses, in seed's ascension, dreams'
burgeoning's becoming Dream,
and senses, in silence suggesting unquestioning love,
a Voice assumably benign—

while trying, like, possibly, everyone else,
to quell a thought that the beautiful confusions of just one
more
   dawn
would give more than any truth or well-intentioned falsehood
can.

Printed in the United States
200986BV00002B/166-192/A

9 781844 714063